DARREN J. DE LEON

Los Angeles | Hinchas Press

Grateful acknowledgement is given to the following publications and journals in which some of these poems and stories first appeared: New Chicano/Chicana Writing (Vol. 1), Cipactli, Mosaic.

Title: The Hoops and Crosses of Mt. Vernon
Description: First Edition.
Los Angeles: Hinchas Press (2025),
Copyright © 2025 by Darren J. de Leon
All rights reserved.
Printed in the United States of America
ISBN: 978-1-954640-09-2
Cover Design: Xicanos For Hire
Cover Photo: Darren J. de Leon
All AI Drawings generated by Xicanos For Hire
Creative ©2025 Darren J. de Leon
Book Design: Xicanos For Hire
Requests for permission to reproduce material from this work should be sent to: Hinchas Press at hinchaspress@gmail.com.
www.hinchaspress.com

CONTENTS

To Be Hard Is To Be A Man Of Truthful Words

Always Forward, Never Backwards

Avoid Digging Your Own Grave

Aztlan
is the first line
in Xicano Poetry

ONLY LOVE CAN CONQUER HATE

K
Mart

Kmart was a towering sign to the west that we could see from our front porch. Located across from the barren field of dirt next to the railing of our dead-end street, the sign was a huge prison guard tower, one big cherry K atop the four blue letters, m-a-r-t. At sunset, the light from the big red K flooded our street before the yellow-orangish street-lamps kicked in. I can't remember our neighborhood without a Kmart or an evening without that colorful sign.

When I was four, I watched the working crew finish the parking lot from atop my father's shoulders, looking at the steamroller creasing the asphalt into flat black sheets. The heat and smoke squirted from the sides of the mammoth iron wheel and out from the back. The Mexican man driving the roller waved towards us as he leaned over the side, stretching to look down onto the slates he was creating. The acrid smell of tar burned my eyes and clogged my nostrils. Looking up towards the brilliant sun, feeling the top of my head heat up, I grabbed my dad's arms which were hoisted above his head. Drips of blood dropped on the back of his neck, splattering on the uncovered dirt of the newly built parking lot. My nostrils filled with a thick warmth that washed slowly down my throat. My father tucked me under his arm and ran me home. I awoke later on the couch with a cold towel over my forehead and my legs propped up by pillows. My dad gave me a sip of lemon iced tea and asked how I was doing?

With the smell of tar still caked to the insides of my nose, my shirt bloodied, my sense of balance warped, I tried desperately to stand up and walk outside to once again see the newborn Kmart. Big enough to fit over 400 customers equipped with baskets and kids and 50 to 75 light blue-smocked employees inside the store. Women lugged around two or three kids on their hip or baby-perched in the baskets' seat, were the lifeblood of Kmart where everything was on sale on small key-coded price tags. On weekends with the store crowded and the parking lot filled, money poured from purses and wallets to checkers who hid the cash in slots or beneath the tray of the cash register like dust swept under a carpet. I would wonder where my dollar bill traveled after I gave it to a cashier, understanding enough that it would go to the armored guards who came twice a day for pickups and then to a bank. But where did it go after that? Since all of my Kmart T-shirts had a Troy, Michigan address on the plastic wrapper, I figured Kmart sent the money to Troy where someone picked it up from the same guards or from inside the U.S. Mail.

When I was six, my parents allowed me to walk to Kmart with

my older brothers and sister to purchase batteries, small toys or look at portable radios. I made the daily summertime trek, sometimes barefooted, to buy a bag of popcorn and a cherry Icee with my vacuuming allowance money. I once got there early enough to watch the guard open the front door with the key and I was the first customer to enter the store, making my way across the cool white tile floor to the snack bar to purchase a cherry Icee—a flavor that was later discovered to have the same carcinogenic red food coloring first found in lipstick. The counter lady recognized my small patch of dark curly hair as I reached up to place my order, speaking into the belly of a red-striped apron.

I remember the guard at the front door who often yelled at me from inside or outside the store for running around without shoes. The guard sat behind a small desk at the front entrance with a beige phone an arm length away on the counter wall behind him. He looked more like a TV bus driver than a guard. When I shopped with my parents on weekends or at night he was never around. Instead a younger and bigger guard, who carried a gun, sat where the old man sat. When I knew he was working, I always behaved inside the store and made sure that I had my shoes on.

In San Bernardino, Kmart was the biggest store in our neighborhood, dwarfing all of the smaller family-owned sporting goods, vacuum cleaner shops, pet stores or specialized shops. These smaller stores became more scarce as people began shopping at Kmart or at the new downtown mall. As I grew older, many of the items we were used to buying at these smaller stores were now being purchased at the larger department stores, which were popping up all the way down the stretch of Route 66 known as Foothill Boulevard, or at

Kmart, my family's favorite. In San Bernardino there were two Kmarts, one located across the field next to my family's house, the other across town next to the housing project everybody called the PJ's.

When I started kindergarten at a Catholic parochial school, my mom took me to a small sporting goods store to buy salt and pepper corduroy school uniform pants. The round balding man with a measuring tape shawled over his shoulders, measured the inside of my leg and around my waist. I looked at myself in the three way mirror with the large oversized cuffed pants. My mother tugged at my waist, checking to see if I would grow into them. My pant legs were cuffed halfway up to my knees, something she would later sew to my size. I liked those pants because all of my brothers had worn the same style. No longer feeling like a child, I grinned happily when my mother signaled an okay to the man. Dashing in and out of the dressing room, I strutted through the stacked aisles with the thick corduroy pants warmly folded in my arms. Those pants were as tough as canvas sails. I wore out three pairs in two years.

Eventually the school changed the dress code, dumping the salt-and-pepper pants and allowing dark blue or black corduroy pants. Soon after, we began buying my school pants from Kmart. Just before the school year was to begin, Kmart would stack the shelves with the dark blue cords. Easy to find with the sizes clearly marked at the base of the shelves, they were always freshly stocked with my awkward size which is longer in the waist than in the length. I never liked the dark blue cords, instead preferring the old standards. Having gotten my pants from the Big K, I was ridiculed by the other schoolchildren for wearing K-Cords. In school, it was easy to tell the difference between Kmart cords and the more expensive Levi's. One had a big K marked on the label and the other ones didn't. My schoolmates somehow figured out that it was a sin to wear Kmart clothes, a clear case of Catholic schoolboy logic; Kmart meant poverty, while mall and Levi's equaled good. It seemed like everybody knew what Kmart clothes looked like while never having admitted to shopping there. When we bagged on one another, we eventually would fall into the hardest bag which usually involved someone's momma living in the PJs, shopping at Kmart or being an "ABC," an African Booty Chaser. The sporting goods store where I had once bought my school pants would eventually close a couple of years later only to be changed into a small Thrifty's Jr. drug store.

Whenever we needed basic items like bath soap, cooking pans, batteries, underwear, socks, we shopped at Kmart. It was the place my brother bought his first guitar. I learned about music by looking at the 8-tracks and albums in the music section. I got most of my clothes there, despite the ridiculing I would take at school. It was the only place, besides Payless, where I could buy the black winos that I liked wearing so much. In my class Lil' Chris and Big Dog Dean, two of the toughest guys in the school, also wore the croquet sac karate shoes, swearing that they made their kicks more powerful and their feet quicker as they tracked down a slower victim in flag football. I liked wearing them because they looked like the shoes Bruce Lee wore in his movies. Since they were light and inexpensive, I could get a new pair sooner. I always like wearing fresh winos.

Many families in the neighborhood also shopped at Kmart. We constantly ran into our neighbors in the aisles, where there was never a clear cut logic on how items or aisles were situated next to each other. Being familiar with all of the store's merchandise, I could tell who shopped there by the small towels or soaps hung in their bathroom. I remember the Gomez family had the same shower curtains that hung in our bathroom. My friend Tino's mom, Concha, worked at Kmart in the kitchen supplies section of the store, restocking pans and blenders. Her family's bathrooms, kitchen, living room and bedrooms looked like a Kmart display. My parents knew many of the older employees, who had worked there for years. Many would talk with my mom, exchanging information about babies and marriages. My mother spent more time conversing with the Kmart employees than she did conversing with our family. My uncle's first girlfriend, Monica, worked as a cashier and smiled and winked at me whenever I went through the checkout lines. I was more familiar with the faces of the Kmart employees than I was with my own blood relatives.

With three boys, one girl and a young uncle who stayed with us, my parents were constantly in and out of Kmart purchasing toys, sports equipment or items used to keep our minds occupied and our bodies out of trouble. My parents got us almost everything we wanted as long as it was within reason, and many times it resulted in Kmart reason. A baseball glove before baseball season was K-reasonable but a horse wasn't. We had a half court basketball key set up in our driveway, both the backboard set and the basketball were purchased as K-goods. We knew that many of Kmart's items were cheaply made, and many times we would want the most expensive items available like the hoop set from the sporting goods in the mall. But the reality of our family's K-income was only as big as a K-Hoop with a lopsided basketball.

One summer, all of the neighborhood kids talked about the new pool on the block, our neighbor's cement pond. My block was made up of predominantly white families with a few kids living on our block. We were the second Mexican family on a dead-end street that was filled with 16 houses, which are currently owned mostly by brown and black families with two white couples living three doors apart. At that time though, the white neighbors had the only pool on our block, but rarely were we invited to swim, instead sneaking into it while they were gone.

Blue concrete, equipped with a diving board and a heated jacuzzi, I could cross the neighbor's pool twice underwater, losing breath while making barrel turns and pushing off to return. It never struck me odd how in the middle of a desert valley there were small concrete containers holding chlorinated water, as if the swimming pool was supposed to emulate the ocean or the beach. That summer my brothers, sister and I were determined to get a pool like the neighbor's but we wanted a longer and deeper one. In San Bernardino, it seemed the more money you had the bigger the pool was at your house. After much whining by us, our father purchased a K-Pool, a small four foot stand up with a plastic lining. My older brothers put it up and together we all helped fill it with water. My mother pulled some old paint from the garage for us to paint pictures on the white aluminum panels of the pool. I painted a picture of a man in a sombrero and bullet belt standing with an Indian warrior. At a backyard barbecue, my uncle, brother and father jumped into the pool at the same time, creating a splash that shot straight up into the night air, swishing water over the sides of the pool. My sister and I did handstands while walking across the bottom of the pool's floor, and played Marco Polo, Sea Hunt, and copied underwater Bruce Lee karate kicks. That pool lasted for four years until after numerous rips in the liner we gave up trying to repair it. On the last time I tried, I was able to swim across the pool eight times underwater before losing breath. Becoming too shallow for diving or cannonballing from the roof of the garage, the pool was surrounded by a forest of weeds which covered our murals. We tore the unused pool down to make room for our new doberman, Budweiser. After I think about it, I can't remember anything from Kmart lasting more than four years.

One year my pony league baseball team, the Cardinals, decided that everyone on the team should get their cleats from Kmart because that year's cleats were white with a red stripe which matched our uniforms. That season more than half the players in the league wore the same exact cleats, even though they didn't match the color of their uniforms. For us it was cleats' destiny. Kmart chose our Cardinal red color for their cleats for a reason. That year we went undefeated in league and went on to compete in All-Star tournaments only to lose in the state final to a team of bald headed cholos from Oxnard wearing the same cleats. After that summer of baseball, I never played organized ball again. Instead, I bought a skateboard.

At the age of thirteen, Kmart was the place where I could practice my skateboarding in preparation for a 200 foot drop in the parking lot of the Ontario Motor Speedways. Having lived next door to a Kmart for 9 years, I'd seen the parking lot slope ever since I was 4 years old. I knew every nook and cranny of the slanted parking lot. Standing in front of the garden section back entrance on top of my silver and black aluminum K-stick with red Cadillac wheels and phony knockoff Gordon Smith trucks from K-Troy Michigan, I made my way down the embankment with a few momentum building kicks. The long asphalt lot was the perfect pitch for a good strong run while making a wide right turn away from Foothill Boulevard. Getting a good amount of speed going down the slope, I flew across the parking lots hundreds of times. On good days the lot would be less than half full and the temperature hot enough to make the asphalt sticky making the turns feel true without the board slipping out from beneath my feet and wiping out. I imagined myself a surfer sliding across a big asphalt wave with cars speeding behind me. After a monumental crash landing from nearly being hit by an irate parker, the manager asked me to never ride in the parking lot again because of "insurance" problems. I stopped for a week until my bruise healed and I headed back out for more. At that time my parents didn't tell me what to do and I sure in hell wasn't going to listen to any K-manager. I eventually practiced enough to feel confident to try the Speedways ramp. On the last day of summer, I tried the drop. On my first attempt, I bailed early, too much speed. I muffed it on the second, I began to wiggle out of control. I found the key on the 3rd attempt, don't go down in a straight line. Instead make wide turns to control your downhill speed. after conquering Ontario I didn't do much downhill skating there or at Kmart, opting to go into the fast paced world of empty pool half pipe or giant tube riding

I grew older and realized that Kmart no longer had the items that I wanted. I had outgrown all of my Kmart clothes and toys just as I had the pool and parking lot. Their record section seemed inadequate and tiny compared to the thirty rows of vinyl, posters, 8-tracks and drug paraphernalia offered at the local record store, Groove Time. Kmart offered G.I. Joe but I wanted Lowrider magazine which was sold only at liquor stores. Kmart had cherry Icees but I had already drank my first six pack of beer by the age of fourteen. I realized that people wanted things and having more things made them feel better about themselves. Kmart offered everything a reasonable person would want at a reasonable price, but they no longer offered me anything I wanted. I no longer felt a need to buy useless items like trendy sunglasses or imitation jeans.

As I changed, so did our neighborhood, and in turn so did Kmart. On the first and the 15th of each month, Kmart was filled with mothers shopping for diapers, baby clothing and toys.

Many people began to get jumped or robbed after shopping there while walking back home. The periphery of the parking lot was filled with used cars for sale. I saw an ambulance haul away an obese lady who had a heart attack inside the store. A group of children laughed at her, joking that she had a heart attack trying to make the blue light special. High school students who were busted for shoplifting had a Polaroid snapshot taken of them for K-Mart's security file and could only get released in the custody of their embarrassed parents. Adult shoplifters were prosecuted to the full extent of the law by the police. My friend EQ got shot selling weed in the alley behind the store. By the time I began cruising with friends, I noticed that each city had their own Kmart located by a freeway, highway or a patch of apartment complexes. Kmart was everywhere. It was like an invisible force that sucked people in and out of the store.

The layout of the store began penetrating my dreams. I dreamt of getting shot late at night in the garden section of the store. In another dream, I paddled my surfboard through the parking lot while catching a wave of potting soil breaking onto Foothill Blvd. I still have one reoccurring dream of walking to the store and with each step I take I bounce a little higher than the previous step until I am catapulting over the sign, slapping the K-tower, pushing off the sign and smashing down into the store like a dropped atomic bomb. When I was eighteen, someone shot out the street lamps on our street and I drank a twelve pack of beer by myself on our porch as the sign's red blanket covered our yard. In a drunken state, I grabbed my golf clubs and began hitting balls at the huge sign in the parking lot. Some of my shots bounced across the lot but none got high enough to strike the Kmart sign. It was too high and far away for me to reach.

On a recent return home to San Bernardino, my father saved a story which appeared in the local paper's Business section about the closing of some local Kmarts, including the one by our house. The closing signaled a nationwide trend for the ailing KCorporation which was shutting down 15 stores and eliminating about 1,300 jobs. According to the story, Kmart did not do a good job managing its bottom line. In contrast, Wal-Mart had become the model of efficiency for today's department stores. But Wal-Mart lacked the character and unpredictability that the Kmart had offered me growing up. In a way, I will miss the local Kmart, not because of the proximity of its location to my parent's house, but the way the store always provided a temporary solution to any predicament or ailment that I found myself in. On occasion, I still crave a cherry Icee on hot days and even though I have a car, there is no Kmart to drive to, no neighboring city, no spacious parking lot filled only at Christmas time, no cool white tiled floor, no logic as why shoe laces were next to napkins, no surfing on garden soil.

KMART, R.I.P.!

A Hat, Cane and Truck

Straw,
brimmed with sweat stains
worn when you drove.
I would pick it up off your bed,
wear and play with it,
looking into the hazy mirror.

From a tree
you said you made it,
smooth, shaved, natural.
Snakes carved into the handle.
It was Wes Parker's bat
when we listened,
the Avenger's umbrella
as we watched,
my gear shifter
when we drove.

Canyon-sized cab,
no radio.
A choke knob,
a Mobil Pegasus keychain
eye level to me.
Me next to you,
Chief and Geronimo.

You are lying down. Sleeping.
You are wearing the coat
from your closet.
Your portrait watches me
watching you.
I reach up,
touch your lips,
your hands,
and the rosary between them.

This Street Does Not Go Through

Dad was born in a house on the other side of town
before where the hospital I was born was built.
His father was born on the outskirts where it's broken down.
I raced in the street and cut corners with a tilt,
Switched direction at the sign which marked the next town.
I knew the speed limits he challenged me to beat.
Limits never conquered because of the length of a dead end street.

He told me to never pull back, to lean into a turn,
because corners are important in making up time or distance.
Momentum will fight me, engines will burn
and draw me away from the corner's chance.
If I fail, the bike will follow physics' dance.
The ground will scratch my knees and heal the next day.
But jeans are cheap and the risk will fade away.

When he was a young man, his father explained the train,
power soon to be antiquated by pistons, oil and gasoline.
I learned strength in a compacted form. He had to explain
how to choke and prep the lawnmower. I wasn't yet a teen.
For thicker lawns, lift all four wheels of the machine.
The thin rotor blades chop the difficult Bermuda.
I listened to the chant and hum of the single piston like Buddha.

An amateur mechanic trained under midnight lamps,
full of torqued timing chains and the metal rods of the gas engine.
That truck ran like a garden, sprouted more wires, circular clamps

for retro fitted pumps, rewired rear tail lights worked in.
Hands the color of our driveway, black tinted skin.
Bigger batteries tightened with a chrome wrench.
In the driveway, I took a burrito break on the workbench.

My dad fixed the garbage disposal frozen by a shredded aluminum can
and potato skins, all the things that can cause it to stop.
He told me to go fast to make up for the time lost over a lifespan.
Don't let time control you. A watch is only a prop.
With an engine you can cut corners on the blacktop.
The faster you become, the more life you will see.
This was the course my father laid out for me.

Visiting the Wondrous Webbers

Ward's garage was his womb of tools,
hanging baby food jars nailed
to a plank, a twist away from a shattering fate,
and I was too afraid to park
my bike inside his marble garage
or walk on his symmetrical lawn.
I was the stranger who parked my thumb
where the three oil marks
blotched the ground next to the chemical cleaners
filed under C. There was no hook
to file my bike across the back beam
where the B's began.

His garage was an engineer's stall with each tool
in its alphabetical place,
buffed and shined to perfection.
Tools ready to eat some wood or conquer the screw.
In my father's garage
everything was either under there or around there.
Humble tools
used to fix and never to create.

When my family ate it was in a TV circle
with the set as the head of the table.
At the Webbers, dinner was church,
file in, pray, swallow the Eucharist.
The same show every night,
June screaming a song of vodka

from a chandelier glass, behind red eyes.
She dealt the rice pilaf like casino cards,
everyone said "amen,"
bowed their heads to chew the potatoes.
I drank water like wine
and wondered why Ricky never slept over my house.

After dinner
Ricky and I listened
to Dr. Demento on the radio,
Ward tried Australia on the shortwave,
June cleaned the stained glass windows
as the 4.0 daughter/head cheerleader practiced splits
with her life-long Lief Garret/Shaun Cassidy goal still intact.

Their war was a race to legal age
or a clean divorce.
A houseful of sprinters lined up to bust out
towards their very own separate hometowns
where a dreamhusband,
a twelve pack,
a new catalog of wrenches and ratchets,
or a younger, hairier lover was waiting
at the finish line.

I could only go home
to fight over Curtis Mayfield 45's
with my brother and sister,
and listen to my mother scold my uncle
over the phone about
getting drunk at last night's wedding.
I would walk around our house

with my eyes closed, turn up the the 8-track,
not knowing that I should say "amen"
whenever I ate early Sunday morning tamales
before mowing the lawn,
say "amen" to no pilaf, no track meet,
while I took a nap
on the brown shag carpet
with tools inside our house, everyday.

My
slippers
look   more
like   my
Dad's with
each
new
day

ONLY A FOO THINK HE WISE

Extra Innings

In front of everybody
Looney likes to lick his ruca Xina's face.
He slid his dust-coated tongue
and puckered his drunk lips
to her pancaked olive skin.
He forced her to shotgun a pisto
and told her to drive us to the store
for more smokes.
Her spider lashes weaved
waves of young lust to us,
as we drank Old Gold
and chain-smoked Camels.

Looney had small shoulders,
almost as narrow as his neck,
good for slipping through window bars,
broken windshields and warped garage doors.
He was the master of the Sunday night beer run.
When kids packed Asteroids with quarters,
and the Stop-n-Go clerk hawked the kids
who ripped out naked scraps of Playboy.
We would park our hoop, the '76 Bullet, around the corner.
Toking a smoke, we'd jam as Looney came booking full
force, smiling and panting as he jumped into
the rolling truck bed full of empties with two twelvers
carried like Easter baskets.

Looney's bottom lip dripped as he talked.
He wanted to go back alone to bang in the Flats.
His blood full of wack, his rag blue
like the graffiti on the corner wall
Burney Hill Counts.
c/s

His eyes held fourteen summers
and had become only scars with raisins hid
inside the slits. He listened to his Tio Reyes
who had no thumbnails and had razored and inked
L-O-V-E H-A-T-E into his knuckles.
He talked about the vato he shot in an Eastside bar after work.
How he learned to throw shoes in the state pinta
and about being in the hole with Pelon from Chinto.
His scar-covered thumb rubbed the chamber
as he handed me a filterless frajo.

I peddled home that night
with a stolen gun in my glove,
my cap flipped backwards,
my cleats hanging from my neck.
I dreamed of naked olive skin and legs,
of speeding life on a red-haired buzz,
of scars on my neck,
of the day of my first shave
and never knowing that to throw bullets
meant you'd have to catch them, too.

To Mohave for Beer

Two days before my twenty-first birthday
mi primo Angel and I unexpectedly left for
Tehachapi to party down with Hector,
our high school buddy, who in our drunken
state we stonedly believed we missed.
With a box of cigs and a case of beer

we flew across midnight roads, throwing empty beers
out the window, peeing under stars, cursing the day-
light, praying for a gas station like the one we missed
a huge neon-lit last chance for gas four
miles back, but ZZ Top was too loud and we were too drunk
to care. Our sole duty was the mission to Hector.

"They start selling again at six." Angel called Hector
from a Mohave 7-11. He said "Bring a case of beer
and we'll celebrate the morning getting drunk
Tehachapi style." He had the next two days
off. But when we arrived we passed out 'till almost four
in the afternoon. In our sleep we missed

the Raiders' game. The bottle caps jingled in my pocket as I missed
the bowl when I peed, but it was okay, Hector
had a lady come in and clean the place. For
dinner, we had breakfast (pancakes, hamburger patties and beer).
I was a confused crusader. "Is it Sunday or Monday?"
We were the lost saturated Knights of Drunk.

Too busy hard rockin' on life and drunk
on AC/DC. In the sun we shot skeets, I couldn't miss,
It was a mustache macho day on the day before my day.
In a field, out of clays, a shotgun-sore shoulder couldn't stop Hector
from shooting tossed cans and bottles of beer
with prison guard accuracy (one, two out of two, three out of three, four..

I was bonding with the earth by not bathing for
the whole mission and staying religiously drunk.
We were in Tehachapi with nothing to do but pound beers
and look at cows eat. I called home and was told that I missed
the party thrown for me. "Who is Hector?
Where in the hell is Tehachapi? By the way, Happy Birthday."

I was lost in the Mohave for what seemed like years. I miss
those drunk days, the spent shotgun shells, Mohave Hector,
showering myself in beer, peeing carefree and forgetting my birthday.

Catching the 22

On the verge of the world becoming stolen,
he turned to face the machine.
The machine turned against the human chains.
The chains locked down the plaza.
The plaza emerged as a sanctuary.
The sanctuary was ignored by the government.
The government told a story of hypocrisy.
The hypocrisy was exposed as a lie.
The lie gave warrant to infiltrating police.
The police shackled thousands of wrists.
The wrists were bruised purple.
The purple knighted the street royalty.
The royalty faced the row of riot police.
The riot police shot tear gas.
The tear gas exploded into rubber bullets.
The bullets hit the veteran's head.
His head was mounted to the newspaper.
The newspaper read like wartime.
Wartime was battled inside bank lobbies.
Bank lobbies harbored the police.
The police versus united.
The united smashed the civilian cameras.
The cameras grew like grass.
The grass was gone from the plazas.
The plazas are now naked.
The now naked follow no leader.
The leaders look into the mirror.
The mirrors reflect the world.
The world sadly breeds in poverty.
Poverty is vulnerable to get rich schemes.
Schemes burgle the world.

THE BRAVEST HOMIE IS THE ONE
WHO CAN CONTROL THEMSELVES

The Teardrop Catcher

"Hey, Rey Rey! Wake up! Ya estuvo! You don't need any more beauty sleep, eh."

Looney snuck his head through my bedroom window by standing on the limbs of the rubber tree plant outside our house.

"Shit! ¿Que onda, foo?" My pillow covered the erection that stood up during my nap. I sat up and looked through the window.

Looney rode his bike across the lawn, jumped off the curb and headed down the street towards sunset, his windbreaker full sail. He screamed "Hey, the rucas are down at the park. Let's go. In and out!" Looney never waited around anywhere for long. 'In and out' was all he ever said about basketball, girls, cars and houses. It was a phrase he'd picked up ever since we watched Clockwork Orange at Huicho's pad.

I hoped to catch a game of basketball down at the black gravel courts, so I grabbed my hightops, reached for my sweatshirt and felt the heaviness of the .38 that Looney's Tio Reyes gave me the night before. This wasn't the first gun I held, but it was mine. I caressed the silver barrel, peeked through the precise holes of the chamber, fascinated by the ease it was to spin the chamber with the slightest of a touch. I took out the sock that I had put the bullets in, picked up the shiny gold cartridges and slowly loaded the gun. I imagined the force that each bullet carried when fired and instantly felt the power of a loaded gun in my hands. I removed three bullets, saving the rest for a later time when I might need them. I grabbed my P.E. gym bag and shoved in another t-shirt, cigarettes and the gun.

I walked down to the park where Looney, Huichol and Small Paul stood around a picnic table passing a forty of 8-ball around. "Que pedo, vato?" said Huichol as he passed the bottle to me. I took a swig and pulled out a cig and lit one up. In the distance, the Pirates and the Cubs were playing baseball game. I had played against both of the sorry ass teams and we had easily beaten them. The Pirates coach looked over at us and shook his head in disgust when he saw me smoking. It was the same look of disappointment when I picked off his son Baby Joe as he tried to steal second base on me. After that game, I remember having beers with Baby Joe at a backyard party. Some of the players in the Pony League went to house parties, but most of them were little momma boys who went home to play with themselves or with video games. Baby Joe was cool. He once had a ditching party at his house where his dad got as drunk as everybody else there. That old fart couldn't coach, but he sure could drink some beer. I could tell he was pissed that he couldn't have a beer in the dugout. I didn't give a fuck what he thought about me.

"Orale, check it out. I cleaned up that gun that Reyes gave me last night. Huichol, you think your brother take us out to the wash to shoot, again? I hope these bullets don't explode. They look awfully old." The gun drooped inside my gym bag and made it tear-dropped shape from its weight as I held it up for all to see.

Looney came over to me and looked into the bag. "Pendejo, my tio said for you to keep that gun at your chante for awhile. You shouldn't have brought it out, estupid. You were supposed to leave it home for a while, ese. Looney looked nervously around the park. The baseball field lights began to hum as they started up for the evening. Huichol silently stared into the setting sun with his eyes squinted when a pack of silhouettes headed towards the bench.

Muñeca and the Primera Locas slowly walked up to us. Muñeca carried a brown paper bag in her arms. Giggles played Brenton Wood and adjusted the volume on the portable radio. Muñeca, with black lips and blue and white streaks of eye shadow flaring from her temples, stepped up on top of the table, reached into the brown sack and pulled a 40 ounce bottle of beer and a 4-pack of Champale like swords from a sheath. "You guys were right, they sell to anyone. Giggles was too scared to buy, so I went in and they sold the stuff to me!" Muñeca proudly twisted the cap off the Champale and stuck a straw in it. She cross eyed her gaze as the straw bounced up and down from the bubbles.

The other girls nervously grabbed a bottle and hid them inside their oversized navy blue windbreakers with arched white Old English lettering spelling out Las Primeras Locas.

Huichol stared at Muñeca as she chugged the Champale. Every time she drank, she got plastered. She gets drunk, then naked and winds up throwing down with the closest horny guy. She liked giving hickeys to vatos in the shape of the letter "M." Every foo hated it. I almost slapped her once when she started giving me a hickey on my stomach. After that, she never showed much interest in me, neither did I with her.

Giggles was the cutest of the girls. She drank but never got drunk, and didn't wear too much makeup. She would give me free nacho chips whenever she worked in the snackbar at the park. "Rey Rey, give me a cigarette, please." She said as she sat on the table next to my gym bag. "Why do you have your gym bag with you? We're not in school."

"I'm ready to play some hoop, but no one is playing, right now, right now.

"What else you got in there?" she tried to grab the bag before I threw my hands around her and squeezed her tight.

"Chica, how 'bout I show you a little bit later, later when there's not so many people around? I can teach you a thing or two." I felt brave and strong in my response. I locked eyes with her. She smelled like bubble gum perfume. Giggles blushed as her eyes slowly fell downward to my chest. For a second, I was holding her up, then she quickly pushed me away from my grip. My blood heavily pumped. I was fully erect. I had a cute girl in my arms, a beer in my hand and an iron in the bag by my side. All of this excitement began to warm up my body. The girl snickered as I tried to wrap my arms around her again, but she was dodgy and coy.

"What's in the bag? Are you gonna show it now or later?" Muñeca said with a coy side-eye. "We want a peek later, too?" said Muñeca's two cousins, Carla and Laura both were 15. Looney was trying to mess with one of them but everytime he got close, they moved further away.

"Rey Rey, give me a frajo. I'll show y'all a trick." Looney put the cig in his mouth.

"Not French bars? We learned those in the sixth grade." Muñeca popped off, "All of the girls do french bars. This ain't no trick, estupid."

Instead, Looney frowned and searched for a light. He grabbed Giggle's cigarette and rolled the cherry over the tip of his. And suddenly snapped his cig into two, put the lit end into his smiling mouth and puffed, pinched his cheek and pulled out an unbroken cig from his mouth. He handed it to me, I inspected it and held up the unbroken unlit cig. We were always amazed by Looney's trick, he's done it a thousand times. I still search the grass for traces of broken cigarettes and there's never any. Looney laughed out loud at everybody's frozen and confused faces.

"Give me a beer!" he demanded.

Muñeca reached inside a bag and pulled out two 8-ball forties. Everybody's lips smacked at the sight of more beer. She laughed and solemnly announced "Pour some out for my dad's oldest friend's son Flaco who was shot two nights ago. He was like my cousin, not my primo, but like my cousin. I think he burned some vato bikers in a drug deal, eh."

Looney and I looked at my bag and then each other. Reyes told us about shooting a vato from Fontana for payback. Flaco couldn't have been more than nineteen.

Small Paul brought more beers and cigarettes. Huichol walked over to the table and placed my gym bag into one of the empty paper sacks. He felt the heaviness of it and didn't say anything. We tossed all the empties and paper bags into the trash-can chained to a tree.

33

"Heads up!" A foul ball comes over towards our table and everybody hunched. The girls put their arms over their heads. Huichol stumbled out in the grass, looked up into the dark sky trying to spot the incoming ball, and walked in figure eights before he settled underneath the foul ball and caught it bare-handed. He slinged over the backstop and the ball went into center field making the second baseman chase the ball. We all laughed and one of the young umpires yelled something at us. We told him to shut up and the coaches of both teams yelled something back to us.

"Fuck this, ese" Looney yelled back grabbing his crotch with one hand and flipping the coaches and umpires with the other. Looney liked to raise his voice and pushed the limits when he gets drunk. Everybody laughed and the game resumed. The score was close in the sloppy game, 17-15. An inside-the-park home run, riddled with throwing errors, tied the game at 17. The centerfielder threw the ball over the backstop trying to nail the runner at home to save the game.

The game finally ended and the snack bar was locked up and the lights turned off. Baby Joe came over to the table in his baseball uniform and asked us, "So, what's the fuckin' deal for tonight? Where's the party?" Huichol's eyes were bloodshot, his words heavy and mumbled. Looking for help, he shrugged his shoulders with both palms facing up.

"It's almost freakin' ten o'clock, Huichol. Me and the girls gotta head home. We all be staying overnight at my place tonight", said Muñeca as she led her drunk girl platoon on their hike home. Giggles blew me a sneaky kiss and waved bye. I slowly nodedd my head in approval and watched her walk away.

Small Paul was asleep on top of the table. Looney rode off on his bike to knock over some trash cans. He always checked for opened car doors. I headed towards the silent basketball court under the streetlamps listening for the sounds of a bouncing ball. A lowered '54 DeSoto scrapes by shooting sparks from the back of the car. Huichol gave a chin up to Nico, one of my brother's friends.

I heard the screech of locked up brakes and a double honk in the distance. Looney came ripping around the corner on his bike heading towards us. A pick-up truck was on his tail following him over the curb and into the park. It was an old man in a cowboy hat with a beard chasing Looney with his truck. Looney entered the baseball field and split across the infield on his bike and out the left field gate, the old in and out. The old man gets out of the truck and runs onto the field carrying a baseball bat, leaving behind his car running with the headlights on. Unnoticed, Huichol slid into the truck and started carving donuts in the middle of the park and sped out of the park to pick up Looney waiting around the corner. That old bastard was yelling like a madman on top of the pitchers' mound, and pointing his bat at Huichol and Looney driving his truck on the sidewalk scraping the side of a brick wall of a trailer park. Huichol drove over a parking post which busted the front grill and a headlight. The madman was running after his truck frantically waving his bat.

Huichol waved to me and Small Paul and we both started to run towards the truck. I hesitated and went back to get the gun inside of the trash can. The silhouette of the old man with the bat started running towards me. Small Paul was sprinting to the truck and jumped in the back of the truck bed.

35

I reached inside the bag, grabbed the gun and dropped to one knee. The darkness turned red and time slowed to a halt. My arm extended and my finger pressed against the slim metal trigger. My arm looked more powerful than it ever has as my thumb cocked back the hammer. I'm detached from my thoughts and the flexing of my hand wrapped around the grip. The bead aimed at the chest of the shadow. I saw the silhouette become larger, but I couldn't see his eyes. He stopped and lifted his hands into the air.

"No! Please don't!"

The huge shadow fell to his knees and buried his face into his hands. My drunken thumb unlocked the hammer. I pointed towards his head and fired and squeezed the trigger. The clack of an empty chamber pierced the silence. The shadow looked up and I saw his eyes buried under the brim of his cowboy hat. He exhaled and fell to the ground. I pointed the gun in the air and pulled the trigger again, another empty clack.

Flashing red and blue lights and screaming sirens lit up the street and woke me up from my freeze. I ran away from the sirens as the police cars jumped over the curbs and entered the park. I turned back and looked at the empty truck smothered against the trailer park wall down the street.

I sprinted like a squirrel on top of walls that border the park and cut across the backyards as barking dogs jumped at my ankles. I ran behind the back of the liquor store and chucked the gun and the bag into a dumpster. I ran across the main highway. Slowly, I walked through the dark, sleeping motel parking lot and jumped over its back fence–dropped into our, my backyard. I slipped into the garage and felt the sting of a cut on my leg, seeing the my blood stained ripped pants.

The distant sounds of police sirens and the acceleration of

engines surrounding the park began to settle into the night. My heart was loudly pumping. I laid back on the bench press. My vision was no longer red. The hum of the circling helicopter beamed down on the neighborhood calmed me down. I lifted the bar and did a quick set of chest presses.

My dad opened the sliding glass patio door and turned the porch light on as the helicopter hovered overhead. He peeked his head through the garage door. "Is everything okay out here? I heard a truck wrecked at the park."

I hid my leg, leaned back and lowered the steel bar onto the bar catch. "Yup. I heard that, too. I was out here lifting when all the racket started up. What happened out there?"

"Some idiot kids stole a truck and rammed it into a wall. You should get inside, it's getting late. Are you sure you're okay?"

"Yeah. "One more set of reps and I'll go inside.""

I watched my dad slide the door shut behind him and cut across the kitchen into the back TV room. I sat up on the bench and looked around the garage for a pack of cigs, I saw my baseball gear, my old baby toys, a lawnmower and a drab olive G.I. duffel bag. My leg stung as I searched for a first aid kit.

I cleared off the pool table and swept the felt clean. I pushed all the dust into the pockets and reached for the triangle rack to set the balls up for a break. After I chalked up my hands and cued my stick, the helicopter finally left.

I finished a game and two stale cigs by myself. On the break, I sank two balls, one solid, one striped. I heard someone jump over the back wall, and in walked Looney into the garage smiling wide carrying a brown paper bag.

"Pool! Cool! Let's get a game going, vato. " Looney handed me a warm bottle of beer. "This was the only crap that I could get my hands on. Beggars can't be choosers, eh!" Looney tossed me a frajo. That fat fucker went after you didn't he, eh?"

"Yeah, I didn't know what the fuck to do. I was ready to shoot that fucker. Where did all the fuckin' juras come from?" I lined up my next bank shot.

Looney turns on the small dusty portable radio. "Music! Ahh, like magic!" He reached into his bag. "You forgot something, ese." He turned around and handed me the gun. It felt like a cold steel teardrop in my hands. I wrapped it inside the duffel bag and hid it in a place I hoped to forget.

Four Notes in Xicano Jazz

I

The hills of Temecula
laden with a cross
watered by tears.

His deed burned
and the ashes blown
into his face.

Spit and fleas
from a horse
mounted by a Stetson.

A shotgun,
a hanging rope
strapped to the saddle.

The minister
smiled
from the foothill.

"There's rail work
in San Bernardino,
Mess-i-can."

Single steps
through orange groves,
eyes over his shoulder.

The Cahuilla pushed
back,
los Californios swept away

from white progress
now called
real estate.

II

The land becomes scarce
generation after generation.
Born into a train town
between Las Vegas and Long Beach,
Big Bear and Hollywood.
Route 66, Tee-Pee Motels,
LBJ as an elevator operator.

Reatas become slave bracelets,
puercos become bullets,
menudo becomes corn flakes,
corridos become Ralphi Pagan,
hogar becomes burning trashcan,
 maíz becomes rubber plants,
pero los nopales y yerba buena
reminds us of nuestra raíces.

III

Indio by birth,
ancient hair,
sequoia-root skin.

A pool of clear water
does not turn pink
from one drop
of red ink.

IV

Freeways
Rain
Reddish-brown skin
Smog
Brake lights
Eagle feather
Heartbeat of a drum
Huitzilpochtli
Green light, Go!
American made steal
Off ramp

Apache Sky
pa' Jose Antonio Burciaga

Beneath a lazy, frayed-denim hemline
raindrops and clouds on your calcos.
Eyelids behind caló frames
of the cholo muralist of Stanford's Casa Zapata.

Tejano horns storm
through a con safos samba
of pachuco skulls and Drinking Cultura.
El Paso is your border lineage.

The weather report reads
"la vida loca."
Your flannel buttoned
to the neck
to keep imperialistic
winds out of the barrio.

Ode to Basketball

To playing 3-on-3,
one-on-one, Action,
H-O-R-S-E,
to running full fives,
or shooting from half court.
To August midnights
in the churchyard
with eyes blinded
by street lamps,
to spring afternoons
on a converted tennis court,
or on the strand at the beach,
with the sun looking over.
To rainy days
playing in a gym,
or in front of a TV,
dreaming of playing
in front of the cameras.
To concrete reality,
playing on asphalt
that makes shoes and hands black,
knees red and ankles sore, or
in a driveway
with a rim
that is too high
and oil stains
on the lop-sided ground.
To dribbling
through the legs,
behind the back,

double pumping,
and the toss that
kisses the white field,
bumps into the orange rail
and engulfs itself through the net.
To Chuck Taylors,
 to bright new leathers,
to old shoes
that are yellowing,
dirty, worn at the soles,
holes in the toes,
to broken laces
never replaced,
to fancy laces looking
like a ladder
or a checkerboard ,
to fat neon strips,
to long ones
wrapped around the ankles,
to bare feet
when playing is unexpected,
making the skin raw,
developing blisters.
To setting screens,
to the pick and roll
that works,
to cherry picking,
to the pump fake,
to the shot topping the key,
to the reverse lay-up,
to bringing it to the hole,
to the no-look pass,

to travelling,
to the hard swat
that bounces the ball
out of bounds,
to the people that watch
and wait for the next game,
their game.
Skunk is at 8-0.
To playing with silent intensity
reaching nirvana,
to the one short guy
among giants,
to the young buck
trying to prove a point,
to the synthetic leather ball
which can be played with
indoors and out,
to the hard-core diehards
compensating their shots
for the wind,
to the kid
with the black heavy metal T-shirt on
and rap-music out of his radio,
to the trash talker
who just lost.
To the ball being
passed around
to hair which becomes wet-heavy
like a sponge.
To soaked shirts
that stick like a second skin.

To chests that fill
with air like balloons,
as hearts pump,
sneakers skid,
the bouncing ball
echoes
off the wall,
as the loose rim shakes,
the chain net rattles,
the nylon net is silent
but snaps as the ball
grips it,
then
falls
through.

A THOUSAND YEARS OF LYING IS WEAKER
THAN ONE DAY OF THE TRUTH

Born on the Third of July

I burned a candle in the shape of Ol' Glory.
I flamed the dried up stars and striped wick,
saw the New York Trash and saxophones burn
and pink condos evaporate in muggy Florida
from boiling swamp waters pissed off by the police.

I cleared a path in the stale wax
for the people forgotten to crawl back into the flame,
build schools and grow their own food
on the land that belongs to everyone.
The flames melted the stars which fell
from the bruised skies into an abused Lake Tahoe
and floated like cheerios for breakfast.
With a spoon I scooped up the napalm stars
and served them up.
a double decker cone,
to a Panther who gave it to a Mohawk
to throw at the Mounties.
What I had burned had always lied to me
so I ripped the stripes off,
and gave them back to the blood banks.
And the blue fields of corn,
I stole them back to feed the hungry victims
because no one has taxed
the fat rich Peter to feed sickly poor Paul.
I burned the red necked South
and its Bible belt used to whip displaced backs.
I scorched Salem and its secret backwoods closets
filled with burnt bones.
I torched L.A. with an aerosol flame thrower

stolen from Axl Rose
after I kicked the shit out of Slash
took his sissy guns
and let the posy roses wilt.
I passed the flame over Utah and wept
over the red rocks, seven caves and three meeting rivers.
Aztlan lost and my history books pried away
with Gatling guns and burnt in the name of God.
Who's God? My gods were not their god.
I smoked every city named after Columbus
because he stole the gold
that left us in shackles
and split us in two by a blade
which turned up in a chota's gun in Oakland.
Like an old useless weed
that greedily sucks up all the water,
I tearfully uprooted this spent wick.
I smashed the candle with the heel of my dancing foot,
one billion pieces of melted red, white and blue wax
crushed beyond recognition.
I gathered the wax with my original energy and hands
and squeezed with all my might,
my arms flexed,
my back strained,
my neck tight,
my shoulders about to break
from the pressure of my grip.
and shaped it into a rock of original tierra.
With the rock in my keffiyeh, I sling it through the museum
window,
and let the spirits run free,
returning the bones to their place,

recovering the culture that existed before.
I reached into the archaeological dig and posted the codices
to the world with the message:
"When you see this world a rockin'
don't come a knockin'
cause I won't be home for Thanksgiving."
The world can hit reply and my number is
1-900-THE-LAND and I live at the top of my soul
right around the corner from my future,
two blocks away from where you live.
And if you have never been to my neighborhood,
it is because you don't live where I live,
you don't see what I see.
I got a poor family and it is much bigger than you.
I've shacked up with my future.
And that measly candle with the stars and stripes
was only good for burning
because all I needed was enough light
to read and teach my kids.
But the stars turned off the electricity
and the money saved went to drop bombs on me overseas.
And the stripes came down on my back
as a tax to bail out the phony failed loans
that left me homeless.
Hey, America! I was teaching my kids
when you turned off the heat and gas.
I was doing all right until I realized
the only thing that trickled down
was my own blood.
I was taking care of my own.
I'd built this big ol' bootstrap
and together we were pulling ourselves up.

And like John Wayne you went crazy on us,
beating us in the middle of the street,
while the world watched,
depositing bullets into our chest,
blaming us for your mistakes.
That candle burned long enough.
It provided enough light
to show us how to make our own candles
for a world not designed for or by us.
My children learned how to read,
and believe my kids are pissed.
Read my lips!
Co-exist or cease to exist.

Prayer of San Andreas Fault

O' Glorious San Andreas,
the archbishop of fault lines.
    Enter the earthquake
        of apostolicity.

We bow our heads,
   run beneath the nearest arch,
   post online before
      your shake ends.
You were the first, San Andreas.
You will be forever St. Andrew,
    second apostle,
    brother of St. Peter,
    fisher of men,
    crucified and displayed in Patras,
    recognized and followed
    by the Lamb of God.

Your direction as simple as a coastland break
Point Delgada to Point Arena,
Point Reyes, Daly City,
and inland through to Berdoo.

We shake as you sing in unity
of the striking of two plates,
a plowed lateral slip
that rocks the State.

Your protection is now called upon.
As you split ranch fences
plot new maps, gapped for slumbered souls
left behind on desert crosses.

We ask you to protect
the quiet fisherman,
the twisted rope-makers,
the humming textile workers,
the dark miners,
the dusty campesinos,
the bloody butchers,
the plump pregnant women,
the gifted soul singer,
and the huddled hands in hospitals.
Bless the igneous people,
the locus,
the ganglion magnitude,
the inflex of grandeur,
the seismic creep,
the stirred and shaken apocalypse,
the bodily convulsion,
the throated fevered mouth,
and the earthly whooping cough.

As your fault sleep
we find your vibration foreign, make
your grumbles holy, beatify
your veins of talc, glorify the exalted
flight of angels, consecrate
your magnitude, divine your tectonic plates.

Teach us to drop and cover,
read the Richter
scale, and surrender
us to you in water
service and canned survival.

May we learn the lesson
of the magnitudes,
and to carry thirtyfold without
complaint so that we may
dip ourselves
in the rubble at the end
of your majestic dance.

Dirty Laundry Full of Blood

Dirty Laundry Full of Blood
NAFTA be your name
thy treaty come
and the Corporation won
in the North
as it is in heaven.

Televised stadium seat
for the 1992 World Series
(N - B - C Sports)
The Ca-na-da-zation of
Joe Carter
3 and 2 count,
the pitcher checks the signs,
and the pitch
Joe Carter
the hardest home run
ever hit in the world
arm-raising Canadian trot
around the American bases
Joe Carter
full of sweet Blue Jay tears
Joe Carter
MVP trophy with a ball on top
Joe Carter
cover of Sports Illustrated
Joe Carter
didn't give a Joe Garagiola ass about
the Mexican flag that hung in Toronto Canada

Toronto
under the dome
una bandera mexicana
in the lonliest left field seats
and "Film at eleven directors"
reframed the shot
and cropped el tri color
from the evening news sports

Who cut the shot
and made Mexico stop
that dropped the soda pop
into the Canadian NAFTA shop

He moved more North
than was needed
more north
as to never be recognized
true north, a salmon
out of water squirming
in his seat
foothold in Canada
to claim the land
in the name of the land
names: Mejica
Mesquakie
Tongva
CheeChaNesh
float beneath
the 10,000 square feet
of slab concrete

How did you get there?
Did you swim?
Walk?
Jump?
Climb?
Sneak?
Phone?
Fax?
Email?
UPS?
Snail mail?
Express?

"I can spot those moving Mex-i-cans
one mile away"

Televised stadium seat,
through gringo landjack
northward bound
narrow-minded tunnels
red necked rivers
a king sized bed of white-sheet rhetoric

Slapped in Temecula
past no points unchecked
100 miles from Hollywood
radical brown chic "RESISTE"
Kathy Lee cries a song
in off, off, off border towns
coffee beans from somewhere

The Mexicans are moving,
cat chased at supreme speed,
Sheriff Dragon and his clan.
El Rio Grande in El Monte
Helicopter documents footprints
counts the blows
one to one-hundred and eighty seven.

Who wants to go shopping for another country?

How does it feel?
To be on your own
No protection at all
Just like a Mexicano in Toronto.

South there is a war
South dead toxin fish
South burning feet
South weekend warrior paint bullets
South headlights from Ford trucks
South plastic bags on feet
South shot by another
South raped by cowboy boots
South below the frontera belt
South metal gallery ducks
South nervous National Guard
South "Chase the nationals!"
South call it training
South floating arms
South dead Christian dollars
South economic easters
South the 3 stooges, Larry, Moe and these United States

South Citibank deposits
South Arnold Palmer golf courses
South asbestos
South Anarchy is a flavor of my gum
South South moving south by south

"The Mexicans are moving,
the problem is
they are moving across the street from me."

Dirty laundry full of blood
a green card with my name.
They gave 187 reasons why
He can justify bullets in their chest.
she must
he must have the house
she must have that house
on top of the hill
He washes ivory hands in rivers
wipes them on dead fish
They spit in the four directions
She eats grapes
He shaves in the mirror
on the back of the bullet
He spins and rinses his clothes in newspaper stands
hangs them to dry
on TV News
conducts a poll
democratically opens our wallet
hands a fiver to La Migra to buy:
more beer sunglasses
jet skis

taxed V8 gas
maquilladora life jackets
Xerox copies of Happy Days
A bellyful of sludge
served on silver platters.

The congregation
the congregation takes the host
the congregation takes the host and quietly files
the congregation takes the host and quietly files into suburban rows.

Dirty Laundry full of blood
another treaty that governs us.
Dirty Laundry full of blood
how long can you hold this game?

To Be Hard is To Be A Man Of Truthful Words

Lawless Prose

There are no laws in poetry
only the word, a prisoner
guilty of a barrage of verbs
sprayed upon the target with ink.
The word this week is "Attica."

There are no laws in poetry
only pen packers flying off
rounds of phrases that pierce
the skull, burrow the brain,
exiting the mouths and fists.

There are no laws in poetry
only the gangsters of page
carrying speared adjectives
and sharply bladed nouns, chucking
knowledge, killing innocence.

There are no laws in poetry
only the fully loaded cannon
of literature triggering the revolution,
destroying the history of lies,
restoring the balance to life.

There are no laws in poetry
only volumes of aggression
needed for oppression. Holy text!
Apart Hate does not read well.
The funniest things happen
when I pull the trigger.

CIA Love (The Agency of Love)
for Gary Webb (R.I.P.)

I

Once upon a time,
there were five young boys.
Each carried a name under their jacket
Smith, Mack, Uzi, Wesson, Beretta.

Their parents too busy working
never an eye out for them,
much too tired to talk about life
or pass on stories.

So the boys roamed,
called themselves Romeo.
Beneath the bridge was their Rome
and between suicide doors,
inside aluminum beer,
through unfiltered frajos.
Travelling from graffiti blocks
to Dipper Drunk Avenue.

The magnum of force in index fingers
trigger dual masks of sorrow,
crease now, hangover later,
white t-shirts, elastic black belts,
white Old English on navy blue.

II

In Hell
I'll crush cans
bring my chemical
sledge
down
one
can
at
a
time

Flatten the aluminum
thin
as
thieves,
disfigure it white
crushed limestone in concrete

I'll bait hearts
hook metacarpals
sustain awake ability
rebirth of energy
a new cool
score a glass pipe
tubes for ungodly use
Distrust the green
consecrate the yayo in backyard tubs

Nothing but my church for you
and a monkey shocked
with federal iron

III

Yellow and blue smoke
parks
grasp my ankles

I walk with flames
shackled
to my legs

I   zombie up
then   zombie down

Midnight scraping paint
from the eaves
barefoot skating
across red ocean carpets

I count the follicles
of unwashed hair
kneel to the sunrise
pray for Wednesday sleep

I am wasted
before Friday
spent matches in a tray
Purchasing shoes in size 9mm
Carrying on conversations
in Yoruba bullets
Depending on masonry walls
for safety

Searching the dusk
of my oily hands
Calculating kegs
Dipping toes into brittle jars
Reading the bottle ten thousand times
collecting the beer labels
laminated to my uncle's liver
Folding aluminum
slick as a silk tie
A rail away from three straight days
Breaking a loki
into 8 balls
100 Franklins bent in my hand
to solve this dilemma of ten thousand bones
First   I'll buy
more sneakers
more T-shirts
knee high socks
below the knee shorts
and fiberglass fenders
Then   I'll buy
chains
an equalizer two turntables
a matching pair of batting gloves
First just lemme get a hit
fold that aluminum
fiddle with the vile
roll the cube between
thumb and palm
flame the gangsta' future
of smoke passing
through brains on eggs

Eyes away from Nicaragua unknown
and Sandino hearts as big as Cuba
The magic of cable tells what time
the ball will drop

Dam the intestines
tickle the black beauty brain
cradle the peanut butter chunks
Separate the cartridge from pen
toss the ball-point
to the curb-side
No need
to document pipe trips
and Van Halen tunnels

As my body becomes a pool
waiting for pearly divers
to crack thru glass tubes

My lungs twist
pecks balloon
pee-wee to Incredible Hulk
of a freebased heart
and games of baseball darts

Saturday crouches like leather on a hog
naked ladies strip by the jacuzzi
500 chi-chis per hour

Dance for a dollar,
 lemme pin this spot
follow the bootylactic

"If you can't hang, you can't hang"

My 18 with a bullet
.45 bullets a week
52 dead each year

Palm Springs   spring break
18 inch woofers will chocolate shake
naked ninjas
and the bootylactic

Make a U
on a one way road
"Went to vacation, left on probation"

IV

My country tis of thee
this is how much they love me
from the C-I-A Agency
land where my people died
from John Wayne's genocide
slaughtered on every mountain side
my shackled freedom pleas

V

Who invented the crack?
The cracker of the whip?

68

Cola sin coke
trusty field of beans
corporate speed
needs to expand

I hide behind diamonds
international trade
tariff traffic
Bible loopholes
syringes ready for exchange

I blew a hole in your nose
as big as   Columbia
Peru y
Panama put together

You'll never escape
the gemly quality of how
my fire works

VI

Who invented the crack?
In this corner playing the neck with a rope,
weighing in with the invention at 220 years...

Look at freeways, veins for vans
which divide the city
pit boulevard against streets
disrupt the unity

of the elder statesmen
propped up
against strip-mall highways
and asphalt without curbs
And in walked crack
fisted dollar bills
and powdered streetcorner greed

Ricky crack corn
and freeways just don't care

The Agency told me
to dress in blue
then red

"A Bahia drug ring
and tons of cocaine
to South-Central LA,
sending profits
to the Contras,
run by the CIA."

Who covers the story?
The ridiculed radio
vibrates in court
outlines online
updated weekly

To never report
conclusions are drawn
like conclusions

VII

Who invented the crack?
The Master of business.

Look what happens to taxes,
Puro profits of a new science.
Chemically endowed and
bibled into believing.

Given the golden instructions
drawn to political metals,
knives with pearl handles,
guns with cross-topped bullets.

VIII

Prison talk
to a third strike owl
God
told me l was a cocaine man
The son
triggered the toilet
The Holy Spirit
had a razor and an aluminum bat

Once a clear
Catholic decision
wisped by my ear
could recite a wind
of verse

Now I
Hopscotch on the rock
of a multiplication table
on a used car lot
Jumped in the accountant
Now I must answer the bag
count puppet movements
vials within numbers.

read my first
each end of the line
mirrors
straws
and spoons

ALWAYS FORWARD, NEVER BACKWARD

Bad Brains at Cal State Long Beach

Rising young men cram the front of the stage
Fluttering booms from the drums jumble bodies into a ring
An angry Rasta crier says "No more Babylon! "
"I no hate, you hate"

Four points of the circle
(Right) Skinhead youth, wearing a peace signed goatee
(Left) Suicidal vato, a bandana across the brow
(Top) A slim, half naked runaway with long hair
(Bottom) Young black man, a blue mohawk splits his head

Inside the pit
drenched with sour sweat, heated by frustration
full of clenched fists and teeth, soaked with saturated guilt
filled with black boots, scars on the strong shirtless backs
And elbows square off as ropes of hair toss in the air

THE BEAT THE BEAT
THE BEAT
THE BEAT
THE
THE BEAT THE BEAT
BEAT

Falling souls are exalted to their feet
a violent halt till the glasses are found
a sacrifice from the pyramid of speakers,
a human bomb to feed the frenzy.
"I and I is forced to live this way."

I'm a brazen bronze chest with brown eyes in a sea of blonde.
I cup my genitals, Throw up my fist, Take a deep breath,
Slam into the pit and join the procession.

Result of the Ring
Guadalupe-Hidalgo Treaty is still broken
400 years of slavery stands uncorrected
Memories of Manzanar
Skanking in a circle on stolen land

Turn Pain Into Power

I

This is the incredible sound
of the earth mourning
          on this aluminum morning
                    crashing down like a wall
as daylight caves into health
as daylight caves into the specific science
                    of photosynthesis

Let's drink to the death
          of this human forest
in the inevitable environmental
          loss of green meaning

Can we write the losses off
          to the chemically endowed
Mountainsides crashing
          twisting the highway into
          the death bow for eternity
Sponge the sun
Unrelaxed carbonates
          inside the lungs
          of Tierra Madre
The greed that brings life
to its limits

II

El Niño as a black day
        with soured rain.
It's gonna rain!
Oulahn! Oulahn! Oulahn!
It's gonna rain!
Reign us down to our knees,
drown our needs
drain the chemicals
        into the sludge
        Slide head first
                4000 miles
        from an ocean home

Spit out the pollution
Make the rounds of revolution
Inbred and dead
        to the dying platoon

Hark! the people from inside
        the earth
        island bronze
        pushing dancing
                feet
                into the ground

Rise above the recycled
        quick solutions
"There is no single African reality"

III

Who keeps the earth in check?
The two guardian eyes
     covered by a shared blindness
plummets into the voided face
     of hypocrisy
Chewing the heart that feeds us
Push down on the pedal
The westernization
     of tropical traffic
Poor, poor Guadalajara!

See this ink that flows through me
They are the tears from the earth
They are trapped in suburban lawns
They are concrete without curbs
They are lonely highways
     that are lonely no more

See that spirit
     that rises within me
It is the glacier that shrinks down
     to the size of a woman/man
       driving a car
It is the spirit of El Niño
     opening for me
     taking coastal cliffs
       for communion
It will sacrifice the insurance
     of white noise

Shut down!
Can't you hear the drum?
The roll of thunder
      from a distant call
           and response
a razor of lighting
      that rips us and the chemically endowed

One Thousandth of A Second

I walked alone across town from Bloomas to Verde for an Elegant Gents' street party. I preferred to walk alone. I didn't have to wait for anybody. If I was late, so what, that's on me. If I was early, I could walk around more. I was that foo that walked the streets at night by themselves. I could keep my own pace, stop and stare in awe at the palm trees in front of the llanteria, make shadow war games on walls lit by street lamps. I feared no one, because everybody feared the lonely figure at night. I could walk in any territory, because those who lived in the shadows knew me, or knew of my kind. I saw better at night. I could spot danger before it spotted me. Dogs see me but don't bark. Cats run from me. When I walk alone, I pretend I'm the last person on earth like in that episode of the Twilight Zone.

As I arrived at the party house, I headed for the familiar lowered ranfla, a baby blue '54 DeSoto parked on the corner of the street. Nico wrestled with his hydraulic batteries in the trunk. I had first met Nico when he got drunk at my house 6 years ago during my brother's graduation party. His little four-year old son played with the leather straps on the steering wheel while sucking on a candystick. I whistled and pounded a hand shake from Nico, who stood proudly behind his car in a newly creased oversized white T-shirt. "Nico! Whassup man?" I slowly pronounced with my teeth clenched.

"Oh Shit! What's the deal, ese?" Nico said. He looked down at me with squinted eyes as he smoked his filterless frajo. "How's your brother? I haven't seen that crazy fuck for a while."

"Oh, Danny? He's alright. ¿Y tu?" I waited to see if he would ask or remember my name. Many just called me Lil' Danny. I rarely told people my name because it was not suave enough. I hated the way Reynoso sounded coming off someone else's tongue.

"Samo, samo. No need to gang bang, nomo. I got mi familia, mi ranfla and a good paying jale at UPS. You walked here, vato?" Nico said.

"Yeah man, so! What's up wit dat?"

"¡Que loco! The Tortilla Flats Locos are on the hunt, ese. Some of the Gents jumped some vatos from the Flats last night. It's safer to stay in, eh. They say them foos are out full force for revenge. Keep your eyes open."

I looked up and down the block. Cruisers had started to roll up and down the street. I didn't see anything out of the ordinary. "So wassup, Nico? Didcha come to check out the party or what?"

"I came to check out the ladies, and the tunes."

"All you solo cholos pour your money into gallons of Amor-all, spoke rims and car batteries. And all you do is stand by your car in front of the party, never entering."

"Aw, nah, ese. Nope. Not all of it is about our cars. You didn't mention the pisto, eh. As long as I got mi chelas on ice, life is smooth, Lil' bro. It don't get better than a can in my hand on my own land." Nico's breath was sour with the smell of beer and cigarettes, his speech slurred and his movement slow. "But I'm still loyal to this soil, ese." He throws his hand towards me to catch a Chicano handshake.

I pointed to my nose, "Nico, this fuckin' nose knows, and its telling me the beer is right here." I quickly pointed to his backseat.

He carefully brought down the trunk hood painted with a mural of a crying Aztec warrior carrying a dead virgin in his arms, and pushed down on the trunk like he was giving CPR. He slowly slid his feet across the asphalt and around the outside of his car. Reaching through the rear window, he turned around and held a beer bottle out to me with the nod of his head and wink of the eye. "Orale, vato. Take one!"

The wet label of the brown bottle easily slid off into my palm. I placed the label on the warm sidewalk to dry out. "Nico, when you gonna go inside?"

"Later man, you know I can't leave my prize out here. Some ese might come around and wanna start fuckin' with it. I gotta take it home. First, I gotta drop the kid off at his abuela's, cover up my car and come back in my dad's truck in a few. I don't want to miss the ladies, whew! There are some fine-lookin' rucas crusin' around tonight, ese. And having the kid with me can only get me so far with the ladies, ya know what I mean" he said as he switched stations on the radio and covered his little boy now fighting sleep on a serape in the front seat.

Nico started singing Daddy's Home to his son.

"Nico, you have an extra frajo, eh?" I fidgeted with my mouth and rubbed my fingers together. Drinking a beer always sets off a nicotine fit. He tosses me a cig. "Graci. You gotta a light?"

"A chela, un frajo and a light? Man, you'll probably want me to smoke it for you too, right." Nico laughed as he pinched the inside of his hip pocket of his chinos feeling for a lighter, "You're too short to be smoking anyway. Each one is a nail in your grave, homie."

"Nico, then you better give me two," I spread my arms apart like Jesus on the cross, "I am always in a hurry to die. I gotta keep on my toes because when the end comes I want to be the first one there to greet it." I figured if I entertained Nico he would choke up another smoke or another beer.

"¡Que loco! Ya me voy, I gotta deliver the kid before the bruja fires up her broom looking for the lil' mocoso."

"You gotta come back, ese, 'Cause I need a ride home after the party, eh." Nico gave me his last two cigarettes in his pack as he pulled away from the curb. The rumble of the muffler shook the street and left a path of heat and exhaust behind it. I tucked one cig behind my ear and lit the other and continued walking up the street illuminated by brake lights of cruisers passing the party. The street was stuffed with cars and began to slow down. All the bombs crawled and slowly squeezed by each other. The drivers' chins nodded up to each other as they passed. Cruisers hopped up and down while their chrome placas in their rear window shot back the headlights' reflections and the sparkles from their metallic murals and pin striped streaks. Funk blasted from the cars. Smiling girls with poofed up hair-helmets hawked the sidewalk looking for the nicest ride hoping to jump inside with a solo rider and cruise the night away.

A large family station wagon full of girls honked at every guy on a motorcycle. I smiled at one of them sitting backwards in the back seat who yelled at me, "Call me in about three years, kid, when you get taller!" I ran towards them, and poked my lit cigarette to their hairspray hard hair. They screamed and tried to dodge my jabs. "Call me again in about three years when your hair grows back." They slapped and pushed my arm out of the rear window. I laughed as I walked away. They were stuck in a cruising traffic jam.

I stood in front of the party house and waited for somebody that I knew so I didn't have to go inside the party alone. I waited for about 5 minutes before Big Gil from the Gents came up to me with a flashlight in his hand. "Eh Rey-Rey, no hanging outside. You gotta go in or get off the street." There was no use in posting up any longer so I walked up to the wrought iron gate of the red brick house to enter. Three of the older Verde Gents frisked me down. "Slam the pisto, eh. No bottles are allowed inside." I slammed it and tossed the brown bottle into a trash container full of empties. I paid the three bucks and received a green stamp with the words 'I'm fucked up' with a picture of a clown with two Xs as eyes. I entered the dark backyard. As I went further in, more of the yard was revealed. Slumped up against a brick wall was a dark familiar figure wearing black corduroy pants, black winos, an oversized black Levi jacket and a red baseball cap flipped up at the bill.

"¿Looney?" I searched the shadow.

Looney slowly picked up his head. His bloodshot eyes strained to see me. His moist bottom lip drooped heavily and kept his mouth open. He slobbered continuously and carelessly.

He stared at me and tried to piece together the puzzle of a familiar voice with an unfocused face. He fell forward trying to pick up his cup of beer. I reached down and helped him up out of the small bush.

"Looney, you alright?" I grabbed his thin arm and placed it around my shoulders holding him upright.

"Rey-Rey is that you? Hey, you gotta help me, carnal. There some levas here that want to throw some chingasos." Looney smacked his lips together as if his mouth was dry. "I think one of their rucas likes the Looney. Ya know, I have that kinda effect on the ladies."

"Looney, who you talking about, man?" I had heard thousands of Looney's wacked out stories before. The angel-dust always made him violently hallucinate. He always tried to sneak a knife or razor into parties with him whenever he smoked dust. His flecha was always somewhere near. I reached into his inside jacket pocket and took out the sharp butterfly knife with thick casings that covered the blade. I placed Looney back against the wall. "Chill here for a minute. I gotta see who's here." I slid the knife into the front pocket of my pants. I was hoping to save Looney from making any foolish mistakes while he was wasted with a knife.

The backyard was solidly filled with people. A six keg mountain dominated the backyard. The fragrance of marijuana, beer and the dark sour secret pockets of PCP filled the air. Two deejays on the opposite sides of the yard had built their forts of gigantic speakers and flashing, spinning multi-colored lights, strobes and horns. I stood in the middle of the yard and two walls of sound crushed me along with the force of packed people flattening me like a tortilla. The knife weighed down my pants. I looked for some backup, just in case anything went down. I spotted Nico entering the party

with the red-headed Vasquez sisters from Verde by his side.
Next door to the party lived my friend Hector who had set up folding lawn chairs with some of his stoner heavy metal buddies on the roof and played an electric guitar through a huge amplifier overpowering the music from the dee-jays. Hector's house overlooked the backyard of the party. The party-goers screamed every time Hector broke into the opening guitar riff of Ozzy's "Crazy Train". The deejays yelled at them to "turn that shit off" through the microphone. They managed to disrupt the music which is what they had wanted to do. In general, everybody noticed them at one time or another. One of the stoners got too drunk to walk and slid off the roof, passing out on the ground. Everybody at the party laughed and chanted "Shut the Fuck Up!" as Atomic Dog filled the dancefloor.

A huge circle formed and a fight broke out between two groups of girls, who rolled around on the ground and punched each other as they scratched each other's face and pulled hair. I recognized one of the fighters as Baby Doll Vasquez who had entered with Nico. She managed to straddle the other girl and began bouncing the other girl's head against the ground. The other girl tried to scratch Baby Doll's face. Out of nowhere, Looney ran into the mix and punched Baby Doll in the back of her head. A couple of the Gent's jumped on Looney and twenty other people joined in to help stop the fight or get in a shot for the hell of it. I looked around for Nico and the flood of people forced me into the pile. I hadn't had any contact for two weeks since the last football game, so I was hungry for pain. I jumped into the dogpile and fell deep into the middle of the scrap. I spotted Looney who clumsily jumped over the backyard wall escaping into the night. Elbows rubbed hard against my face and pierced my sides. Somebody slugged me in the throat and pushed my legs over my head causing me to go deeper into the pile. The knife slid out of my pockets and hit me in the chin and fell to the ground. Light started to appear through the cracks of bodies and I frantically searched for the knife while I was upside down. I straightened myself upwards and went to my knees looking through the legs and grass for the white-pearl casing. The crowd was pushed outside as the dee-jay announced the party was over and everyone had to leave. I continued to lay on the ground while everybody piled off and headed out of the party to continue fighting out in the street. I couldn't find Nico anywhere.

"Hey ese, everyone gotta take a hike, man. The party is over." A shadow extended its hand to help me up.

I rubbed the dirt off my elbows. "What do ya mean! I just got here, I didn't even get a beer."

"Hey, Rey-Rey! Aw ese, come back in an hour, the keg will be flowing again then." The faceless voice was Big Gil who walked towards the back of the yard.

In the front of the house, the street was jammed and I saw flares blocking off the street about two blocks down, but I didn't see any cops. Some vato was yelling in the middle of the street with blood on his shirt, his partners pushed him into a red Candy Apple Monte Carlo car with a broken window and moved quickly down the street honking as they went. Three of the Verde Gents ran after them with baseball bats, catching up to them and smashing the sides of the car while throwing punches at the driver and the passengers.

I climbed the ladder that was leaning against Hector's house. Hector and the stoners had finished rolling three joints and handed me the fattest one as I walked up the pitch of the roof. "Hey, hey, Rey-Rey what do you say?"

"Give me a lighter and I'll start the smoking today." I responded without missing a beat. We got stoned on top of the roof under the stars as all hell broke loose below in the street. The whole block was well lit from the helicopter circling above. The shining eye-in-the-sky peered down on the street and along the block quickly clearing out. The eye in the sky left, once all calm returned.

An hour later, we were still stoned on the rooftop. Hector was playing Stairway to Heaven on an acoustic guitar as his mom told us to come down from the roof and get inside. From up there, we could see the Verde Gents sitting around a keg in the back yard after all the empty foam cups had been picked up and the dee-jays were loaded and gone. I jumped down from the roof and walked to the front of the house with dry-mouth and a thirst in search of quenching. An old truck pulled up to the curb and the window rolled down I looked around for some of the Gents and a voice yelled at me "Lil' Danny whassup?"

"Nico," I was relieved. "You got any smokes?"

"Símon, I got some with me, lemme park. I don't want to cruise around in this old jalopy, eh." He parked his dad's work truck and got out and lit a cig while handing me one. "Wasn't that a pretty cool bronca?"

"I thought it was fucked up. Those locas you came in with got into a scrap and ended the party."

Nico looked confused, "Nobody got hurt, except some crazy foo from the Flats who crashed the party. He got his nose busted on. The Gents chased them outta here".

I searched my pockets for my leño, "Hey man, wanna hit some mota, I gotta a joint."

"Naw man, no need for drugas anymo'. I got the future to

look after, man. Ya know mi familia, mi ranfla, mi jale. Beers, that's all I need. Hey Lil' Danny, looky. I found a cool flecha inside, ese." Nico reached into the cab of the truck and pulled out a cold beer and handed it to me.

"Yeah, I lost my knife inside, a white pearl butterfly about six inches."

"No shit! Then I guess I found it. That's a cool knife, ese. I've been playing around with it since I left the party." He twirled it in his hand like a baton, opening it and closing it rapidly. "I like this butterfly, it reminds me of the old days." He spun it around like Bruce Lee, folded it shut and tossed it to me.

I felt guilty that I lied to Nico about it being mine. It would have been better if he kept it. Looney didn't need another knife, all it did for him was cause more trouble. "I think I left my leño on the roof. I'll be right back." I headed back to the top of the roof where Hector was wrapping up an extension cord to his amp.

From on top, I saw the herd of Gents at their watering hole around the kegs, telling war stories and counting the money from the door. I could see Nico parked in the front of the house searching for a station and tunes. Hector was rolling a joint with a dollar bill. A car pulls up to Nico and three guys get out and start talking to him. Hector is almost finished rolling the joint. Nico reaches into the back of his truck and begins to swing a broomstick at the guys. They begin hitting him over the head with beer bottles. One of them opens his trench coat and a shotgun appears on his side like a sword.

The standoff between the opened trench coat and Nico as skinny as the broomstick that he held lasted quicker than a blink of the eye. The gun released a thunderous flash and clap. Nico flew backwards like he was yanked by an invisible rope. His body was snatched and separated from his soul which remained standing in shock. His body crumbled in the middle of the street like a slab of meat both flesh and bones exposed to the open night.

The trench coat held up the short barrelled shotgun like a torch. He calmly spat on the ground and turned around and slowly entered the backseat of the car, which backed up over Nico's body. As they sped away, they yelled "Los Flats Locos, Y-Que!" The Gents stopped their grazing around the keg and ran to the front of the house. I jumped off the roof with Hector following me.

I ran to Nico only to find a pile of meat and clothing in the middle of the street. Nico's face briefly appeared and his eyes began to flutter wildly. His eyes stopped and looked through us, beyond our club jackets, beyond the gravel barrio, beyond the painted murals, beyond the hovering moon and the farthest star. His appearance changed as he laid on the ground, wrinkles and cracks developed in his face. His hands grew bigger as they clutched each other and melted into one. He yelled and his voice soared higher and higher to a stinging pitch that made our ears bleed even though they were covered by our beer soaked hands. His eyes ignited flames that created an incredible heat that burned our hair, singed our eyebrows and melted all of our clothes off, scorching our body hairs and desires of peace.

I tried to reach out to Nico but the heat pushed me away. We chained our arms together tried to save Nico's body from slowly sinking into the ground as the earth violently shook, and the sun touched the earth for one thousandth of a second and hid back in its space in the galaxy. He sat up, looked around as the flames spread across all the streets of Barrio Verde and burned all the trees and melted all the asphalt and tar, turning the sidewalks black from the char.

Nico was gone. Nico wasn't the one that should have died. I knew it. The Gents knew it. Hector knew it. Our bodies were burnt to a crisp yet we were still flesh filled with invisible ash. Darkness reappeared and a bright red bloodstain was forever embedded into the spot where Nico's body had fallen.

I crawled home alone and cried all the way. The Gents didn't have any more parties. Hector stayed off the roof and Verde became a barrio with deep shades of sadness and emptiness filling every crevice, staining every soul like a tattoo on the face. The sun refused to shine on Verde for 100 years, offering only humbling darkness and absolute silence. All the loud lively voices were forever muffled from the shame of a lost son.

Avoid Digging Your Own Grave

Blood From The Sun

I

When the Kmart parking lot was first built,
I flew on Papa's back, like a feather
from an eagle's wing soaring through the wind.
A Mexican man rode giant rollers,
ironed out tarry thick asphalt pages
flat like the properly creased Catholic
straight lines of my salt and pepper school pants.
Waves of tar smoke coated my throat, the sun
stroked me, my nose filled with bloody mucus.
From the ground I was lifted by my wrist,
my dad carried me like a touchdown run,
his voice an ambulance siren. Ichor
tattooed the sidewalk. I wanted brilliance
to shine upon us, a father and son.

II

Then, K-Mart became shelter from boredom
Skateboarding, Cherry Icees, shoplifting
chanclas for Mother's Day. Summer teen bum,
no more model car kits, just barefooting.
Heart attack jokes about dying in line,
a parking lot for a dime bag of weed.
Alive at night, sleeping in the sunshine,
posted up, I sold an eightball of speed.
When the bullet hit Loncy's head it bleed

from the back. When the bullet struck my hip
my dad was at work. All I saw was red
and blue lights. I took an ambulance trip.
"I'm sixteen." Gurney metal. "I don't know."
Light in my pupil. My words become slow.

III

I.C.U. bed dreams
the tar smell of parking lots
the flight of eagles

IV

My life swims upstream
clear tubes and bags of IV
slowly drips downstream

From Pinball to Phoenix

Friday night began by plowing
through a box of Marlboro reds,
a caguama of 8 ball, a finely
rolled leño of Mohican, playing
pinball on one quarter, popping games,
selling them two for a quarter, fishing
for beer, bumming smokes.

The baseball field lights shut
down as curtains go to bed beneath
the Santa Anas and stars. Prophetic
whistles announce la chota as they roll
by, street dogs looking for bone or scrap.
Bodies shrink into bushes, mop-lean
behind trees, dip behind walls or
drown into shadows.

House parties are local, small,
warm and one dollar. Tiny mixes
from the kitchen counter,
slices P-Funk salads, scorches
Furious Five steaks.
Her young wide hips mesmerize me
through my buzz, soft elbows
float, tight curls bounce
on her back, she moves
like poured water
and drinks Champale
from a bottle.

I go outside for a square, search for a bush,
for relief, and gather the hero in me
to open up, ask her for a dance,
cut the rug and get wet with
warm salty water.

Pelon cruises by
in a familiar '64,
tells me about slumbering nighties
with wine, I take a hit
from a fresh bowl, work diamonds
on the hydraulics, balance the beer
between my legs.

I've smoked myself sober, look
into the flip-down mirror, eyes
red as Gargantua, breath
the color of tobacco,
body funk from dodging la jura,
 beer stains on my shirt.

I'm wasted,
fourteen, a disfigured child with a big nose,
oceans away from the shore of manhood .
Too short to drive, too tall for a bike
My creased cords are flat,
grass stains on my leather hightops.
I have no code, no map, no compass
to find the state of responsibility where
I am to dwell.

I slouch riding shotgun,
throw the seat back
and see the streams of Phoenix
rise from the pit of an ashtray.

The Agency Said to Dress in Blue, Then Red

I grew up poor in L.A., and then Rialto.
Pushed out of school to sling cocaine.
Crashed a stolen car and broke my elbow.
Missed my court date, urine dirty with Mary Jane.

Freeway runner since my summer of 19.
Caught a case, possession of a gram of coke.
By 22, gold watch, Cuban link and diamond pinky ring.
Inside my closet full of cash, I'll never be broke.

God told me, "I was a snow king type."
Crack gave birth to zombies with bare feet.
A woman left her children for the pipe.
Once in prison, my name disappeared on the street.

No visitors, no letters, just burpees and I wait
for my countdown to begin or a new court date.

Darren J. de Leon's Bio

Darren J. de Leon is an award winning poet from San Bernardino, California. He was one of the editors of *TLACUILX: Quarantined Tongues* (Hinchas Poesía Press) and co-producer of the *Project 1521 Podcast*. In 1996, he co-founded Los Delicados: Poetas del Sol, San Francisco's avant garde leaders of the Latine Spoken Word scene. His work has appeared in various publications including *New Chicano/Chicana Writings* (University of Arizona Press), *Word Descarga* and *Raza Spoken Here* (Calaca Press); Cipactli, and Fourteen Hills. He produced and hosted KUCR's Radio Aztlan in Riverside, and Radio 2050 at KPFA in Berkeley, CA. Currently, he co-produces *RAMA Blueprints Podcast* and is an avid bicyclist.

www.ingramcontent.com/pod-product-compliance
Lightning Source LLC
Chambersburg PA
CBHW051223120626

46547CB00013B/1479